THE
FAITHFUL
PROMISER

THE
FAITHFUL
PROMISER

By

John MacDuff

Bottom of the Hill Publishing
Memphis, TN
www.BottomoftheHillPublishing.com

ISBN: 978-1-61203-774-5

John MacDuff

Content

John MacDuff

*"He has given us His **very great and precious promises**!"* — 2 Peter 1:4

"He who has promised is faithful." — Hebrews 10:23

It has often been felt a delightful exercise by the child of God, to take, night by night, an individual *promise* and plead it at the mercy-seat. Often are our prayers pointless, from not following, in this respect, the example of the sweet Psalmist of Israel, the *royal promise-pleader*, who delighted to direct his finger to some particular "word" of the Faithful Promiser, saying, *"Remember Your promise unto Your servant, upon which you have caused me to hope."* — Psalm 119:49

The following are a few gleanings from the *Promise Treasury* — a few "crumbs from the Master's Table," which may serve to help the thoughts in the hour of closet meditation, or the season of sorrow.

John MacDuff

PARDONING GRACE

"Come now, let us reason together," says the Lord. *"Though your sins are like scarlet, they shall be as white as snow; though they are red as crimson, they shall be like wool."* — Isaiah 1:18

My soul! your God summons you to His audience chamber*! Infinite purity* seeks to reason with *immense vileness! Deity* stoops to speak to *dust!* Do not dread the meeting. It is the most *gracious* — as well as most *wondrous* of all conferences. Jehovah Himself breaks silence! He utters the best tidings a lost soul or a lost world can hear, "God is in Christ reconciling the world unto Himself, not imputing unto men their trespasses." What! Scarlet sins, and crimson sins! and these all to be forgiven and forgotten! The just God "justifying" the unjust! — the *mightiest* of all beings, the *kindest* of all!

Oh! what is there *in you* to merit such love as this? You might have known your God only as the "consuming fire," and had nothing before you except "a fearful looking for of vengeance!" This gracious conference bids you to dispel your fears! It tells you that it is no longer a "fearful thing," but a blessed thing to fall into His hands! Have you consented to His overtures? Until you are at *peace* with Him, *happi-*

11

ness must be a stranger to your bosom.

Though you have all else beside, if bereft of God — you must be bereft indeed! Lord! I come! As your *pardoning grace* is freely offered, so shall I freely accept it. May it be mine, even now, to listen to the gladdening accents, "Son! Daughter! be of good cheer! Your sins, which are many — are all forgiven!"

NEEDFUL GRACE

"As your days — so shall your strength be." —
Deuteronomy 33:25

God does not give grace — *until* the hour
of trial comes. But when it does come — the
amount of grace, and the nature of the special grace required, is granted. My soul! do not
dwell with painful apprehension on the *future*.
Do not anticipate coming sorrows; perplexing
yourself with the grace needed for future emer-
gencies; tomorrow will bring its promised *grace*
— along with tomorrow's *trials*.

God, wishing to keep His people humble, and
dependent on Himself, does not give a *stock of
grace*; He metes it out for every day's exigencies,
that they may be constantly traveling between
their own emptiness — and Christ's fullness;
their own weakness — and Christ's strength.
But when the exigency comes, you may safely
trust an *Almighty arm* to bear you through!

Is there now some "thorn in the flesh" sent
to lacerate you? You may have been entreat-
ing the Lord for its removal. Your prayer has,
doubtless, been heard and answered; but not
in the way, perhaps, either expected or desired
by you. The "thorn" may still be left to goad, the
trial may still be left to buffet; but "more grace"
has been given to endure them. Oh! how often

have His people thus been led to glory in their infirmities, and triumph in their afflictions — seeing that the power of Christ rests more abundantly upon them! The strength which the hour of trial brings — often makes the Christian wonder to himself!

ALL-SUFFICIENT GRACE

*"God is able to make **all grace** abound toward you; that you, always having **all sufficiency** in **all things** — may abound to every good work."*
— 2 Corinthians 9:8

All-sufficiency in all things! Believer! Surely you are "thoroughly equipped for every good work!" Grace is no scanty thing, doled out in pittances. It is a glorious treasury, which the *key of prayer* can always unlock — but can never empty. It is a *fountain* — full, flowing, ever flowing, over flowing!

Mark these *three ALL'S* in this precious promise. It is a three-fold link in a golden chain, let down from the throne of grace by the God of grace. "All grace!" "all-sufficiency!" in "all things!" and these to "abound." Oh! precious thought! My need cannot impoverish that *inexhaustible treasury of grace!* Myriads are hourly hanging on it, drawing from it — and yet there is no diminution. Out of that fullness we, too, may all receive, "grace upon grace!"

My soul, do you not love to dwell on that *all-abounding grace?* Your own insufficiency in everything, met with a divine "all-sufficiency in all things!" Grace in all circumstances and

15

situations, in all vicissitudes and changes, in all the varied phases of the Christian's being. Grace in sunshine — and in storm; in health — and in sickness; in life — and in death! Grace for the old believer — and the young believer. Grace for the *tried* believer, and the *weak* believer, and the *tempted* believer. Grace *for* duty — and grace *in* duty; grace to carry the *joyous* cup with a steady hand — and grace to drink the *bitter* cup with an unmurmuring spirit; grace to have *prosperity* sanctified — and grace to say through tears, "May Your will be done!"

COMFORTING GRACE

"I will not leave you comfortless: I will come to you." — John 14:18

Blessed Jesus! How Your presence sanctifies trial; takes loneliness from the chamber of sickness; and the sting from the chamber of death! Bright and Morning Star! Precious at all times, You are never so precious as in "the dark and cloudy day!" The bitterness of sorrow is well worth enduring — to have Your promised consolations.

How well qualified, Man of Sorrows, are You to be my Comforter! How well fitted to dry my tears — You who shed so many Yourself! What are my tears — my sorrows — my crosses — my losses, compared with Yours, who shed first Your *tears*, and then Your *blood* for me! Mine are all deserved, and infinitely less than I deserve. How different, O Spotless Lamb of God — those pangs which rent Your guiltless bosom!

How sweet those comforts which You have promised to the comfortless, when I think of them as flowing from an *Almighty Fellow Sufferer*, "A brother born for adversity" — the "Friend that sticks closer than any brother!" — one who can say, with all the refined sympathies of a holy exalted human nature, *"I know your sorrows!"*

John MacDuff

My soul! calm your griefs! There is not a sorrow you can experience but Jesus, in His treasury of grace — has an exact corresponding solace: "In the multitude of the sorrows I have in my heart — Your comforts delight my soul!"

RESTRAINING GRACE

"Satan has desired to have you — that he may sift you as wheat. But I have prayed for you — that your faith may not fail." — Luke 22:31, 32

What a scene does this unfold!

Satan tempting — Jesus praying!

Satan sifting — Jesus pleading!

"The strong man assailing" — "the stronger than the strong" beating him back!

Believer! here is the past history and present secret of your safety in the midst of temptation. An *interceding Savior* was at your side, saying to every threatening wave, "Thus far shall you go — and no farther!" God often permits His people to be on the very *verge* of the precipice, to remind them of their own weakness; but never farther than the brink! The *restraining hand* and *grace* of Omnipotence is ready to rescue them, "Although he stumbles — yet he shall not be utterly cast down." And why? "For the Lord upholds him with His right hand!"

The wolf may be prowling for his prey; but what can he do when the almighty Shepherd is always there, tending with the watchful eye that "neither slumbers nor sleeps!" Who cannot subscribe to the testimony, "When my foot slipped, Your mercy, O Lord! held me up!" Who can look back on his past pilgrimage, and fail to see it crowded with *Ebenezers*, with this inscription: "You have delivered my *soul* from death, my *eyes* from tears, and my *feet* from falling!" My soul, where would you have been this day, had you not been "kept" by the power of God?

"Hold me up — and I shall be safe!" Psalm 119:117

RESTORING GRACE

"I will heal their backsliding!" — Hosea 14:4

Wandering again! And has He not left me to perish? Stumbling and straying on the dark mountains, away from the Shepherd's eye and the Shepherd's fold — shall He not leave the *erring wanderer* to the fruit of his own ways, and his *truant heart* to go hopelessly onward in its career of guilty estrangement?

"My thoughts," says God, "are not as your thoughts, neither are your ways My ways."

Man would say, "Go, perish! ungrateful apostate!"

God says, "Return, O backsliding children!"

The Shepherd will not, cannot, allow those sheep to perish, whom He has purchased with His own blood! How wondrous His forbearance towards His wandering sheep! — tracking its guilty steps, and not ceasing the pursuit until He lays the wanderer on His shoulders and returns with it to His fold rejoicing! My soul! why increase by farther departures, your own distance from the fold? Why lengthen the dreary road your gracious Shepherd has to traverse in bringing you back? Do not delay your return! Do not provoke His patience any longer!

Do not venture farther on forbidden ground! He waits with outstretched arms to welcome you once more to His tender bosom! Be humble for the past, trust Him for the future. Think of your former backslidings — and tremble! Think of His patience — and be filled with holy gratitude! Think of His promised grace — "and take courage."

SANCTIFYING GRACE

"Being confident of this very thing — that He who began a good work in you will carry it on to completion until the day of Christ Jesus!" — Philippians 1:6

Reader! Is the good work begun in you? Are you *holy*? Is *sin* being crucified? Are your heart's *idols* abolished, one by one? Is the *world* less to you — and *eternity* more to you? Is more of your Savior's image impressed on your character; and your Savior's love more enthroned in your heart? Is Salvation to you, "the one thing needful?" Oh! take heed! There can be no *middle ground*, no standing still; or if it is so, your position must be a false one.

The Savior's blood is not more necessary — to give you a *title* to Heaven; than the Spirit's work — to give you a *fitness* for Heaven. "If any man has not the Spirit of Christ — he is none of His!" *Onwards!* should be your motto. There is no *standing still* in the life of faith. "The man," says Augustine, "who says 'Enough,' that man's soul is lost!"

Let this be the superscription in all your ways and doings, *"Holiness to the Lord!"* Let the admonishing word exercise over you its habitual power, "Without holiness, no man shall see the Lord." Moreover, remember, that to be *holy* —

is to be *happy*. The two are equivalent terms. Holiness! It is the secret and spring of the joy of angels; and the more of holiness attained on earth — the nearer and closer my walk is with God — the more of a sweet pledge shall I have of the bliss that awaits me in a holy Heaven. Oh! my soul, let it be your sacred ambition to "Be Holy!"

REVIVING GRACE

"But those who wait upon the LORD shall renew their strength; they shall mount up with wings as eagles! They shall run — and not be weary; and they shall walk — and not faint." — Isaiah 40:31

"Will You not revive us, O Lord?" My soul! are you conscious of your *declining* state? Is your walk less with God, your affections less heavenly? Have you less conscious nearness to the mercy-seat, diminished communion with your Savior? Is prayer less a privilege than it has been? Are the pulsations of spiritual life more languid, and fitful, and spasmodic? Is the bread of life less relished? Are the seen, and the temporal, and the tangible, displacing unseen and eternal realities? Are you sinking down into this state of drowsy self-contentment, this conformity of your life with the world, forfeiting all the happiness of true religion and risking and endangering the better life to come? Arise! Call upon your God! *"Will you not revive us, O Lord?"*

He might have returned nothing but the withering repulse, "How often would I have gathered you — but you were not willing!" "Ephraim is joined to his idols — let him alone!" But "in wrath, He remembers mercy." "They shall revive as the corn." "The mouth of the Lord has spoken it." How and where is reviving grace to be found? He gives you, in this precious promise, the *key*. It is on your bended knees — by a return to your deserted and unfrequented prayer-chamber! "Those who wait upon the Lord!" "Wait on the Lord; be of good cheer, and He shall strengthen your heart; wait, I say, on the Lord!"

PERSEVERING GRACE

"The righteous shall hold on his way." — Job 17:9

Reader! How comforting to you amid the ebbings and flowings of your changing history — to know that the change is all with you, and not with your God! Your spiritual vessel may be tossed on *waves of temptation*, in many a dark midnight storm. You may think your Pilot has left you, and be ready continually to say, "Where is my God?"

But fear not! The ship which bears your spiritual destiny, is in better hands than yours! A *golden chain of covenant love* links it to the eternal throne! That chain can never snap asunder. He who holds it in His hand gives you this as the pledge of your safety, "Because I live — you shall live also!"

"Why are you then cast down, O my soul? and why are you disquieted within me? hope in God!" You will assuredly ride out these stormy surges, and reach the desired haven! But be faithful with yourself: see that there is nothing to hinder or impede your growth in grace. Think how little may retard your progress. One *sin* indulged — one *temptation* tampered with — one *bosom traitor* — may cost you many a bitter hour and bitter tear, by separating between you and your God. Make it your daily prayer, "Search me, O God, and know my heart; test me and know my anxious thoughts. Point out anything in me that offends You, and lead me along the path of everlasting life!"

DYING GRACE

"I have the keys of hell and of death!" — Revelation 1:18

And from whom could dying grace come so welcome — as from You, O blessed Jesus? Not only is Your name, "The Abolisher of Death;" but You Yourself have died! You have sanctified the grave by Your own presence, and divested it of all its terrors.

My soul! are you at times afraid of this, your last enemy? If the rest of your pilgrimage-way is peaceful and unclouded, does there rest a dark and portentous *shadow* over the *terminating portals?* Fear not! When that dismal entrance is reached — He who has the keys of the grave and of death suspended at His golden belt, will impart grace to bear you through!

Death is but the *messenger of peace* — it is your Savior calling for you! The promptings of nature, when, at first, you see the darkening waves, may be that of the frightened disciples, when they said, "It is a ghost! and cried out for fear!" But a gentle voice will be heard high above the storm, *"It is I! Do not be afraid!"* Death, indeed, as the wages of sin, must, even by the believer, be regarded as an *enemy.* But, oh! blessed thought, it is your *last* enemy — the cause of your last tear! In a few brief moments after that tear is shed — and your God will be wiping every vestige of it away! "O Death! where is your sting? O Grave! where is your victory? Thanks be unto God, who gives us the victory through our Lord Jesus Christ!" Welcome, vanquished foe! Birthday of Heaven! "To die is gain!"

AFTER
GRACE — GLORY

"The Lord will give grace — and glory!" —
Psalm 84:11

Oh! happy day: when this toilsome warfare
will all be ended — Jordan crossed — Canaan
entered — the multitude of enemies of the wilderness no longer dreaded — sorrow, sighing,
death, and, worst of all, sin, no more either to
be felt or feared! Here is the *terminating* link in
the golden chain of the everlasting covenant. It
began with *predestination;* it ends with *glorifi-
cation.* It began with sovereign grace in eternity
past, and no link will be lacking until the ransomed spirit is presented faultless before the
throne!

Grace — and glory! If the *pledge* is sweet —
then what must be the *reality?* If the wilderness
table contains such rich provision — then what
must be the glories of the eternal banqueting
house? Oh! my soul, make sure of your saving
interest in the grace — as the blessed prelude
to glory. "Having access by faith into this grace,
you can rejoice in hope of the glory of God;" for
"whom He justifies — those He also glorifies!"

Has grace begun in you? Can you mark —
though it should be but the drops of the begin-

31

ning *streamlet* which is to terminate in such an *ocean* — the tiny grains which are to accumulate and issue in such "an exceeding weight of glory?" Do not delay the momentous question! The day of offered grace is on the wing! "No grace — no glory!"

ANOTHER COMFORTER

"And I will ask the Father, and He shall give you another Comforter, that He may abide with you forever!" — John 14:16

Blessed Spirit of all grace! how often have I grieved You! resisted Your dealings, quenched Your strivings; and yet You are still pleading with me! Oh! let me realize more than I do — the need of Your gracious influences. Ordinances, sermons, communions, providential dispensations, are nothing without *Your life-giving power!*

"It is the Spirit who quickens." "No man can call Jesus, Lord — but by the Holy Spirit." Church of the living God! is not this one cause of your deadness? My soul! is not this the secret of your languishing frames, repeated declensions, uneven walk, and sudden falls — that *the influences of the Holy Spirit are undervalued and unsought?* Pray for the outpouring of this blessed Agent for the world's renovation, and your own. "I will pour out My Spirit on all flesh," is the precursor of millennial bliss!

Jesus! draw near, in Your mercy, to this dull heart, as You did of old to Your mourning disciples, and breathe upon it, and say, *"Receive the Holy Spirit."* It is the *mightiest* of all blessings; but, like the sun in the heavens, it is the *freest* of all, "For if you, being evil, know how to give good gifts unto your children; how much more shall your Father in Heaven give the Holy Spirit unto those who ask Him!"

PROVIDENTIAL OVERRULING

"And we know that all things work together for good to those who love God; to those who are the called according to his purpose." — Romans 8:28

My soul! be still! You are in the hands of your Covenant God! Were all the strange circumstances in your history the result of *accident*, or *chance* — you might well be overwhelmed! But "all things," and this thing (be what it may) which may be now disquieting you — is one of these "all things" that are so working mysteriously for your good. Trust your God! He will not deceive you — your interests are with Him in safe custody.

When *sight* says, "All these things are against me," let *faith* rebuke the hasty conclusion, and say, "Shall not the Judge of all the earth do right?" How often does God hedge up your way with thorns — to elicit *simple trust!* How seldom can we *see* all things so working for our good! But it is better discipline to *believe* it. Oh! for faith amid frowning providences, to say, "I know that Your judgments are good;" and, relying in the *dark*, to exclaim, "Though He slays me — yet will I trust Him!"

Blessed Jesus! to You are committed the reins of this universal empire. The same hand that was once nailed to the cross — is now wielding the scepter on the throne, "all power in Heaven and in earth is given unto You." How can I doubt the wisdom, and the faithfulness, and love, of the most mysterious earthly dealing — when I know that the *Scroll of Providence* is thus in the hands of Him who has given the mightiest pledge Omnipotence could give — of His tender interest in my soul's well-being, by giving Himself for me?

SAFE WALKING

*"All the **paths** of the LORD are mercy and truth — unto such as keep His covenant and His testimonies."* — Psalm 25:10

The *paths* of the Lord! My soul! never follow your own paths. If you do, you will be in danger often of following *sight* rather than *faith* — choosing the evil, and refusing the good. But "commit your way unto the Lord — and He shall bring it to pass." Let this be your prayer, "Show me Your ways, O Lord; teach me Your *paths*." Oh! for Caleb's spirit, "to wholly follow the Lord my God" — to follow Him when *self* must be sacrificed, and hardship must be borne, and trials await me. To "walk with God" — to ask in simple faith, "What would You have me to do?" — to have no will of my own — but this, that God's will is to be my will. Here is safety — here is happiness!

Fearlessly follow the *Guiding Pillar*. He will *lead* you by a right way, though it may be by a way of hardship, and crosses, and losses, and privations — to the city of God. Oh! the blessedness of thus *lying passive in the hands of God*, saying "Undertake for me God!" Oh! the blessedness of dwelling with holy gratitude on past mercies and interpositions; trusting these as pledges of future faithfulness and love; and hearing His voice behind us, amid life's many perplexities, exclaiming, "This is the way — walk in it!" "Happy," surely, "are every people who are in such a case!" It will be for you, Reader, if you can form the resolve in a strength greater than you own: *"This God shall be my God forever and ever; He shall be my Guide even unto death!"*

LOVE IN CHASTISEMENT

*"As many as I **love** — I rebuke and chasten."*
— Revelation 3:19

Sorrowing Believer! what could you wish more than this? Your *furnace* is severe; but look at this assurance of Him who lit it. Love is the *fuel* that feeds its flames! Its every *spark* is love! It is *kindled* by your heavenly Father's hand — and *designed* as a pledge of His special love. How many of His dear children has He so rebuked and chastened; and all, all for one reason, "I *love* them!" The myriads in glory have passed through these *furnace-fires* — there they were chosen — there they were purified, sanctified, and made "vessels fit for the Master's use;" the *dross* and the *alloy* purged — that the pure metal might remain.

And are you to claim *exemption* from the same discipline? Are you to think it strange concerning these same fiery trials that may be *purifying* you? Rather exult in them — as your *adoption privilege.* Do not envy those who are strangers to the *refining flames —* who are "without chastisement."

You should surely rather have the severest discipline — with a Father's love; than the fullest earthly cup — without that Father's smile. Oh! for grace to say, when the *furnace* is hottest, and the *rod* sorest, "Yes, Father, for this was Your good pleasure!" And what, after all, is the severest of your *chastisements*, in comparison with what your *sins* have deserved? Do you murmur under a Father's correcting love? What would it have been to have stood the wrath of an un-propitiated Judge, and that, too, forever? Surely, in the light of eternity, the heaviest pang of earth — is indeed "a light affliction!"

A CONDITION IN CHASTISEMENT

"If need be!" — 1 Peter 1:6

Three gracious words! Not one of all my *tears* has been shed for nothing! Not one *stroke of the rod* has been unneeded — or might have been spared! Your heavenly Father loves you too much, and too tenderly, to bestow *harsher correction* than your case requires!

Is it loss of health — or loss of wealth — or loss of beloved friends? Be still! there was *a needs be!* We are no competent judges of what that "needs be" is; often through aching hearts we are forced to exclaim, "Your judgments are a great deep!" But God here pledges Himself, that there will not be one *unnecessary thorn* in the believer's crown of suffering. No *burden* too heavy will be laid on him; and no *sacrifice* too great will be exacted from him. He will "temper the *wind* — to the shorn lamb."

Whenever the "need be" has accomplished its end — then the *rod* is removed, the *chastisement* suspended, and the *furnace* quenched.

"If need be!" Oh! what a pillow on which to rest your aching head — that there is not a *drop* in all your *bitter cup* — but what a God of love saw to be absolutely necessary! Will you not *trust*

His heart — even though you cannot trace the mystery of His dealings? Not too curiously prying into the "*WHY* it is?" or "*HOW* it is?" — but satisfied that "*SO* it is," and, therefore, that all must be well!

STRENGTH IN THE WEAK

"He will not break a bruised reed, and He will not quench a smoldering wick!" — Matthew 12:20

Will Jesus accept such a heart as mine? — this erring, treacherous, vile heart? The PAST — how many forgotten vows — broken covenants — prayerless days! How often have I made new resolutions, and as often has the reed succumbed to the first blast of temptation!

Oh! my soul! you are low indeed — the things that remain, seem "ready to die." But your Savior-God will not give you "over unto death." The *reed* is bruised — but He will not pluck it up by the roots. The *wick* is reduced to a smoldering ember — but He will fan the decaying flame.

Why wound your loving Savior's heart — by these repeated declensions? He *will* not — *cannot* give you up! Go, mourn your weakness and unbelief. Cry unto the *Strong* for strength.

Weary and faint one! You have an *Omnipotent arm* to lean on. "He never grows faint or weary!" Listen to His own gracious assurance: "Do not be afraid — for I am with you. Do not be discouraged — for I am your God. I will strengthen you and help you. I will hold you up with My victorious right hand!" Leaving all your false props and refuges, let this be your resolve, "I will trust in the Lord always, for the Lord God is the eternal Rock!"

ENCOURAGEMENT TO THE DESPONDING

"All whom the Father gives Me — will come to Me; and whoever comes to Me — I will never cast out!" — John 6:37

Cast out! My soul! how often might this have been your history! You have cast off your God — might He not often have cast out you? Yes! cast you out as *fuel for the fire of His wrath* — a sapless, fruitless cumberer! And, notwithstanding all your ungrateful requital for His unmerited forbearance — yet He is still declaring, "As I live, says the Lord, I have no pleasure in the death of him who dies!" Your sins may be legion — the sand of the sea may be their befitting type — the thought of their vileness and aggravation may be ready to overwhelm you; but be still! your patient God waits to be gracious! Oh! be deeply humbled and softened because of your guilt, and resolve to dedicate yourself anew to His service, and so coming, He will by no means cast you out!

Do not despond by reason of *former shortcomings* — your *sins* are great — but your *Savior's merits* are greater! He is willing to forget all the past, and sink it in oblivion, if there is present love, and the promise of future obedience.

"Simon, son of Jonah — do you love Me?" Ah! how different is *God's* verdict from man's! After such sins as yours, man's sentence would have been, "I will cast him out!" But "it is better to fall into the hands of God, than into the hands of man;" for He says, *"I will never cast out!"*

PEACE IN BELIEVING

"Peace I leave with you; My peace I give you. I do not give to you as the world gives. Do not let your hearts be troubled and do not be afraid." — John 14:27

"You will keep him in *perfect peace* — whose mind is stayed on You." "Perfect Peace!" What a blessed attainment! My soul! is it yours? I am sure it is not — if you are seeking it in a perishable *world*, or in the perishable *creature*, or in your perishable *self.* Although you have all that the world would call enviable and happy, unless you have peace *in* God, and *with* God — all else is unworthy of the name — a spurious thing, which the first breath of *adversity* will shatter, and the hour of *death* will utterly annihilate!

Perfect Peace! What is it? It is the peace of *forgiveness.* It is the peace arising out of a sense of God reconciled through the blood of the everlasting covenant — resting sweetly on the bosom, and the work of Jesus — committing your *eternal all* to Him.

My soul! stay yourself on God, so that this blessed peace may be yours. You have tried the *world.* It has deceived you. Prop after prop of earthly scaffolding has yielded, and tottered, and fallen! Has your God ever done so? Ah! this false and *counterfeit worldly peace* may do well for the world's day of prosperity. But test it in the hour of sorrow; and what can it do for you when it is most needed? On the other hand, what though you have no other blessing on earth to call your own? You are *rich indeed* — if you can look upwards to Heaven, and say with an unpresumptuous smile, "I am at peace with God."

BLISS IN DYING

"Blessed are the dead who die in the Lord." — Revelation 14:13

O my soul! is this blessedness yours in prospect? Are you ready, if called this night to lie down on your death-pillow, sweetly to fall asleep in Jesus?

What is the *sting* of death? — It is sin. Is death, then, to you, robbed of its sting, by having listened to the gracious accents of pardoning love, "Be of good cheer, your sins, which are many, are all forgiven!" If you have made your peace with God, resting on the work and atoning blood of His dear Son, then the *Last Enemy* is divested of all his terror, and you can say, in sweet composure, of your dying couch and dying hour, "I will both lay down in peace and sleep — because You, Lord, make me to dwell in safety!" Reader! ponder that solemn question, "Am I *ready* to die? Am I living as I should wish I had done — when that *last hour* arrives?"

And when shall it arrive? Tomorrow is not yours. Truly, there may be but a *step* between you and death! Oh! solve the question speedily — risk no *doubts* and no *perhaps*. Every day is proclaiming anew the lesson, "The race is not to the swift nor the battle to the strong." Seek to live, so that that hour cannot come upon you too soon, or too unexpectedly. *Live a dying life!* How blessed to live — how blessed to die — with the consciousness, that there may be but a *step* between you and glory!

A DUE REAPING

"In due season we shall reap — if we faint not." — Galatians 6:9

Believer! all the glory of your salvation belongs to Jesus — none to yourself! Every *jewel* in your eternal crown is His — *purchased* by His blood, and *polished* by His Spirit. The confession of time — will be the ascription of all eternity: *"By the grace of God I am what I am!"* But though "all is of grace," your God calls you to personal strenuousness in the work of your high calling — to "labor," to "fight," to "wrestle," to "agonize;" and the *heavenly reaping* will be in proportion to the *earthly sowing*: "He who sows sparingly — shall also reap sparingly; and He who sows bountifully — shall also reap bountifully!" What an incentive to holy living, and increased spiritual attainments!

My soul! would you be a star shining high and bright in the skies of glory? Would you receive the *ten-talent* recompense? Then do not be weary. Put on your *armor* for fresh conquests. Be daily gaining some new *victory over sin*. Deny yourself. Be a willing cross-bearer for your Lord's sake. Do good to all men as you have opportunity; be patient under provocation, "slow to anger," resigned in trial. Let the world take knowledge of you — that you are wearing Christ's *uniform*, and bearing Christ's *spirit*, and sharing Christ's *cross*. And when the *reaping time* comes, He who has promised that the cup of cold water cannot go unrecompensed, will not allow you to lose your reward!

AN END OF WEEPING

"The days of your mourning shall be ended!"
— Isaiah 60:20

Christ's people are a *weeping band* — though there is much in this lovely world to make them joyous and happy. Yet when they think of sin — their own sin, and the unblushing sins of a world in which their God is dishonored — need we wonder at their tears? Are we surprised that they should be called "Mourners," and their pilgrimage home a "Valley of Tears?" *Sickness, bereavement, poverty* and *death* following the track of sin — add to their mourning experience; and with many of God's best beloved, one tear is scarce dried — when another is ready to flow!

Mourners! rejoice! When the *reaping* time comes — the *weeping* time ends! When the *white robe* and the *golden harp* are bestowed — every remnant of the *sackcloth attire* is removed. The moment the pilgrim, whose forehead is here furrowed with woe, bathes it in the crystal river of life — that moment the pangs of a lifetime of sorrow are eternally forgotten!

Reader! if you are one of these careworn ones, take heart — the days of your mourning are numbered! A few more throbbings of this aching heart — and then sorrow, and sighing, and mourning, will be forever past! "He will wipe every tear from their eyes. There will be no more death or mourning or crying or pain!"

Seek now to mourn your *sins* — more than your *sorrows*; reserve your bitterest tears for forgetfulness of your dear Lord. The saddest and sorest of all bereavements, is when the sins which have separated you from Him, evoke the anguish-cry, "Where is my God?"

A SPEEDY COMING

"Behold, I come quickly!" — Revelation 3:11

"Even so! come, Lord Jesus!" "Why do the wheels of Your chariot tarry?" For six thousand years, this world has rolled on, getting time-worn with age, and wrinkled with sins and sorrows. A waiting Church sees the long-drawn shadows of twilight announcing, "The Lord is at hand!" Prepare, my soul, to meet Him! Oh! happy day, when your adorable Redeemer, so long dishonored and despised, shall be publicly enthroned in the presence of an assembled universe, crowned Lord of All, glorified in His saints, satisfied in the fruits of His soul's travail, destroying His enemies with the brightness of His coming — the lightning-glance of wrath — causing the hearts of His exulting people to "rejoice with joy unspeakable and full of glory!" Prepare, my soul, to meet Him!

Let it be a joyous thought to you — your "blessed hope" — the meeting of your *Elder Brother!* Stand oftentimes on the *watchtower* to catch the first streak of that coming brightness, the first murmur of these chariot wheels. The world is now in preparation! It is rocking on its worn-out axle. There are voices on every side proclaiming "He comes! He comes to judge the earth!" Reader! are you among the number of those who "love His appearing?" Remember the attitude of His expectant saints: "Blessed are those servants whom the Lord, when He comes, will find WATCHING!"

EVENING LIGHT

*"At **evening** time — it shall be light!"* — Zechariah 14:7

How inspiring is the thought of coming glory! How would we rise above our sins, and sorrows, and sufferings — if we could live under the power of "the world to come!" — were *faith* to take at all times its giant leap beyond a soul-trammeling earth, and remember its brighter destiny — if it could stand on its Pisgah Mount, and look above and beyond the mists and vapors of this *land of shadows*, and gaze on the "better country." But, alas! in spite of ourselves, the *wings of faith* often refuse to soar — the spirit droops — guilty fears depress — sin dims and darkens — God's providences seem to frown — God's ways are misinterpreted — the Christian belies his name, and his destiny.

But, "At evening time — it shall be light!" The material sun, which wades through clouds and a troubled sky, sets often in a couch of lustrous gold! So, when the *sun of life* is setting, many a ray of light will shoot across memory's darkened sky, and many mysterious dealings of the wilderness will then elicit an *"All is well!"* How frequently is the presence and upholding grace of Jesus especially felt and acknowledged at that hour, and griefs and misgivings hushed with His own gentle accents, "Fear not! It is I! Do not be afraid."

A triumphant deathbed! It is no unmeaning word; the *eye* is lit with holy luster, the *tongue* with holy rapture, as if the harps of Heaven were on it. My soul! may such a *life's evening time* be yours!

HEAVENLY ILLUMINATION

"You do not realize now what I am doing — but you will understand hereafter." — John 13:7

As the natural sun sometimes sinks in *clouds* — so, occasionally, the Christian who has a bright rising, and a brighter meridian, *sets* in gloom. It is not always "light" at his evening time; but this we know, that when the *day of immortality* breaks, the last vestige of earth's shadows will forever flee away! To the closing hour of time, *Divine Providence* may be to him a *baffling enigma;* but before the first hour has struck on Heaven's clock — all will be cleared up! My soul! "in God's light you shall see light." The *Book of His decrees* is a *sealed* book now, "A great deep" is all the explanation you can often give to His mysterious ways. The *why* and the *wherefore* — He seems to keep from us — to test our faith, to discipline us in trustful submission, and lead us to say, *"May Your will be done!"*

But rejoice in that *'hereafter'* — light awaits you! *Now* we see things imperfectly as in a cloudy mirror — but *then*, face to face! In the great *mirror of eternity* — all the events of this chequered earthly scene will be reflected; the *darkest* of them will be seen to be bright with mercy — the severest dispensations, "only the severer aspects of His love!" Pry not, then, too curiously! Do not judge too censoriously on *God's dealings* with you. Wait with patience, until the *grand day of disclosures*; one confession shall then burst from every tongue, *"He has done all things well!"*

A GLORIOUS REUNION

"I will come again, and receive you unto Myself; that where I am, there you may be also!" — John 14:3

If the meeting of a long absent friend or brother on earth is a joyous event — then what, my soul, must be the joy of your union with this Brother of brothers, this Friend of friends!

"I will come again!" Oh! what an errand of love, what a promised honor and dignity is this — His saints to share, not His *Heaven* only — but His *immediate* presence! "Where I am — there you shall be also!"

"Father, I will" (It was *His dying wish* — a wondrous addition in that testamentary prayer) "that those whom You have given Me be with Me where I am." Happy reunion! Blessed Savior, if Your presence is so sweet on a sin-stricken earth, and when known only by the invisible *eye of faith* — then what must be that presence in a sinless Heaven, unfolded in all its unutterable loveliness and glory!

Happy reunion! it will be a meeting of the whole ransomed family — the *Head* with all its members — the *Vine* with all its branches — the *Shepherd* with all His flock — the *Elder*

Brother with all His kinsmen. Oh, the joy, too, of mutual recognition among the *death-divided ties* snapped asunder on earth — and now indissolubly renewed — severed friendships reunited — the triumph of love complete — love binding brother with brother, and friend with friend, and all to the Elder Brother! My soul! what do you think of this Heaven? Remember *who* it is that Jesus says shall sit with Him upon His throne, "He who *overcomes!*"

EVERLASTING ESPOUSALS

"And I will betroth you unto Me forever!" — Hosea 2:19

How wondrous and varied are the *figures* which Jesus employs to express the tenderness of His covenant love! My soul! your Savior-God has **married you!** Would you know the *TIME* of your betrothal? Go back into the depths of a by-past eternity, before the world was; then and there, your espousals were contracted: "I have loved you with an everlasting love!"

Soon shall the bridal-hour arrive, when your absent Lord shall come to welcome His betrothed bride into His royal palace! The *Bridegroom* now tarries — but see that *you* do not slumber and sleep! Surely there is much all around, demanding the girded loins and the burning lamps. At "midnight!" (the hour when He is least expected) the cry may be — shall be heard, "Behold, the Bridegroom comes!"

My soul! has this mystic union been formed between you and your Lord? Can you say, in humble assurance of your faith in Him, "My beloved is mine — and I am His!" If so, great, unspeakably great — are the glories which await you! Your dowry, as the bride of Christ — is all

63

that *Omnipotence* can bestow — and all that a glorified bride can receive! In the prospect of those glorious nuptials, you need dread no pang of widowhood. What God has joined together, no created power can put asunder! He betroths you, and it is, "forever!"

A JOYFUL RESURRECTION

"The trumpet will sound, the dead will be raised imperishable, and we will be changed! For the perishable must clothe itself with the imperishable, and the mortal with immortality!" — 1 Corinthians 15:52-53

Marvel of marvels! The sleeping ashes of the sepulcher — springing up at the blast of the archangel's trumpet! The dishonored dust — rising into a glorified body, like its risen Lord's!

At the time of *death*, the **soul's** bliss is perfect in *kind*; but this bliss is not complete in *degree*, until reunited to the *tabernacle* it has left behind to mingle with the sods of the valley. But tread lightly on that grave — it contains precious, because ransomed, dust! My *body*, as well as my *soul* — was included in the redemption price of Calvary! And "those also who sleep in Jesus — will God bring with Him." Oh! blessed Jubilee-day of creation, when Christ's "dead men shall arise!" The summons shall sound forth, *"Awake, and sing — you who dwell in the dust!"*

All the joys of that resurrection morn — we cannot tell; but its chief glory we do know, "When He shall appear, we shall be *like* Him;

for we shall *see* Him as He is!" LIKE Him! My soul, are you waiting for this manifestation of the sons of God? Like Him! Have you caught up any faint *resemblance* to that all-glorious image? Having this blessed hope — are you *purifying* yourself, even as He is pure? Be much with Jesus now — that you may exult in meeting Him hereafter. Thus taking Him as your Guide and Portion in life, you may lay down in your dark and loathsome grave — and look forward with triumphant hope to the dawn of a resurrection morn, saying, "And when I wake up — You are still with me!"

A NIGHTLESS HEAVEN

*"And the city has no need of sun or moon — for the glory of God illuminates the city, and **the Lamb is its light!**"* — Revelation 21:23

*"There shall be **no night** there!"* — Revelation 21:25

My soul! is it night with you here? Are you wearied with these midnight tossings on life's tumultuous sea? Be still! The day is breaking! Soon shall your Lord appear! "His going forth is prepared as the morning." That *glorious appearing* shall disperse every cloud, and usher in an eternal noontide which knows no twilight. "The sun will never set; the moon will not go down. For the Lord will be your everlasting light. Your days of mourning will come to an end!" *Everlasting light!* Wondrous secret of a nightless world! — the glories of a present God! — the everlasting light of the *Three in One*, quenching the radiance of all created orbs — superseding all material luminaries!

"My soul waits for the Lord — more than those who watch for the morning!" The *haven* is nearing — star after star is quenched in more glorious effulgence! Every bound over these *dark waves* is bringing you nearer to the eternal shore! Will you not, then, humbly and patiently endure "weeping for the night," in the prospect of the *eternal joy which comes in the morning?*

Strange realities! A world without night! A heaven without a sun! And, greater wonder still, *yourself* in this world — a joyful citizen of this nightless, sinless, sorrowless, tearless Heaven! — basking underneath the Fountain of uncreated light! No exhaustion of glorified body and spirit to require repose; no lassitude or weariness to suspend the ever-deepening song, "Worthy is the Lamb, who was slain, to receive power and wealth and wisdom and strength and honor and glory and praise!"

A CROWN OF LIFE

"And when the chief Shepherd shall appear, you shall receive
a crown of glory that fades not away." — 1 Peter 5:4

What! is the beggar to be "raised from the ash-heap, set among Princes, and made to inherit a throne of glory?" Is dust and ashes, a puny rebel, a guilty traitor — to be pitied, pardoned, loved, exalted from the depths of despair, raised to the heights of Heaven — gifted with kingly honor — royally fed — royally clothed — royally attended — and, at last, royally crowned? O my soul, look forward with joyous emotion to that day of wonders, when He whose head shall be crowned with many crowns, shall be the dispenser of royal diadems to His people; and when they shall begin the joyful ascription of all eternity, "Unto Him who loved us and washed us from our sins in His own blood, and has made us Kings — to Him be glory and dominion forever and ever. Amen."

Will you not be among the number? Shall the princes and monarchs of the earth wade through seas of blood for a corruptible crown; and will you permit yourself to lose the incorruptible diadem, or barter it for some perishable nothings of earth? Oh! that you would awake to your high destiny, and live up to your transcendent privileges as the citizen of a Kingly Commonwealth, a member of the Blood-royal family of Heaven. What would you not sacrifice, what effort would you grudge, if you were included in the gracious benediction, "Come, you blessed of My Father, inherit the kingdom prepared for you from the foundation of the world?"

THE VISION AND FRUITION OF GOD

"Then I heard a loud voice from the throne: Look! God's dwelling is with men, and He will live with them. They will be His people, and God Himself will be with them and be their God! He will wipe away every tear from their eyes. Death will no longer exist; grief, crying, and pain will exist no longer, because the previous things have passed away. Then the One seated on the throne said: Look! I am making everything new! Write, because these words are faithful and true." — Revelation 21:3-5

Glorious consummation! All the other glories of Heaven are but dim emanations from this all excelling glory. Here is the focus and center to which every ray of light converges. God is "all in all."

Heaven without God! — it would send a chill of dismay through the burning ranks of angels and archangels; it would dim every eye, and hush every harp, and change the whitest robe into sackcloth!

And shall *I* then, indeed, "see God?" What! shall *I* gaze on these inscrutable glories — and live? Yes, God Himself shall be with them, and be their God! They shall "see His face!" And not only the vision — but the *fruition*.

Oh! how does sin in my holiest moments, damp the enjoyment of Him! It is the "pure in heart" alone who can "see," far more — who can "enjoy" God. Even if He did reveal Himself now, these eyes could never endure His emanating brightness.

But then, with a heart *purified* from corruption — a world where the taint of sin and the power of temptation never enters — the soul again a bright mirror, reflecting the lost image of the Godhead — all the affections devoted to their original high destiny — the love of God the *motive principle*, the *ruling passion* — the glory of God the *undivided object* and *aim* — the will with no opposing or antagonist bias — man will, for the first time, know all the blessedness of his chief end: "to glorify God, and to enjoy Him forever!"

Printed in the USA
CPSIA information can be obtained
at www.ICGtesting.com
LVHW011547090524
779753LV00018B/167